Produce Manager

Workers YOU Know

Produce Manager

Angela McHaney Brown

RSVP RAINTREE
STECK-VAUGHN
PUBLISHERS

A Harcourt Company

Austin   New York
www.steck-vaughn.com

Published by Raintree Steck-Vaughn Publishers,
an imprint of Steck-Vaughn Company

Art Director: Max Brinkmann
Editor: Pam Wells
Design and Illustration: Proof Positive/Farrowlyne Associates, Inc.
Planned and Produced by
Proof Positive/Farrowlyne Associates, Inc.

Library of Congress Cataloging-in-Publication Data

Brown, Angela McHaney.
    Produce manager/Angela McHaney Brown.
        p. cm. — (Workers you know)
    Summary: Introduces the job of produce manager in a supermarket,
describing the duties and responsibilities of this occupation.
    ISBN 0–8172–5594–X
        1. Vegetable trade—Management—Vocational guidance—Juvenile literature.
    2. Fruit trade—Management—Vocational guidance—Juvenile literature.
    3. Produce trade—Management—Vocational guidance—Juvenile literature.
    4. Grocery trade—Management—Vocational guidance—Juvenile literature.
    [1. Produce trade. 2. Grocery trade. 3. Occupations.] I. Title. II. Series.

HD9225.A2 B76 2000
381'.148—dc21
                                                                                        99–051703

Printed and bound in the United States
1 2 3 4 5 6 7 8 9 0 LB 03 02 01 00

Acknowledgments:
Photo Credits: **6:** © David Young-Wolff/Photo Edit; **8:** © David Young-Wolff/Photo Edit; **10:** © David Young-Wolff/Photo Edit; **12:** © David Young-Wolff/Photo Edit; **14:** © David Young-Wolff/Photo Edit; **16:** © David Young-Wolff/Photo Edit; **19:** © David Young-Wolff/Photo Edit; **21:** © David Young-Wolff/Photo Edit; **22:** © David Young-Wolff/Photo Edit; **24(lt):** © David Young-Wolff/Tony Stone Images; **24 (rt):** © David Young-Wolff/Photo Edit; **24(b):** © Mark Segal/Tony Stone Images; **24–25:** © David Young-Wolff/Photo Edit; **27:** © David Young-Wolff/Photo Edit; **29:** © David Young-Wolff/Photo Edit; **31:** © David Young-Wolff/Photo Edit

Note: You will find more information about
becoming a produce manager on the last page of this book.

What do you think about when you go to the supermarket? Do you imagine how to mix fruits and vegetables to make a tasty salad? Maybe one day you will be a chef in a restaurant. Do you think about what foods are good for you to eat and what foods are not? Maybe one day you'll become a nutritionist (new-**tri**-shun-ist), someone who helps people with special needs figure out what foods would be best for them to eat. Or, maybe you like to look at the bright colors of fruits and vegetables and feel the different textures of their skins. If you do, perhaps you'd like to make piles of produce into beautiful displays, and answer questions about how to use different fruits and vegetables—like me.

I'm a produce manager in a supermarket. The produce section is the area where you can find fresh fruits and vegetables, like broccoli and bananas.

Hi, I'm Maria Sanchez, one of the managers in this grocery store. My job is to organize all the fresh fruits and vegetables. I have several people who work with me. But we are just part of the large staff of workers in the store.

Maria Sanchez
Produce Manager

6

I am responsible for all the fresh fruits and vegetables in the store. One part that I really enjoy is making the display shelves and bins look inviting. I want customers to see how colorful these fruits and vegetables are! Then, they will buy more to take home and enjoy. After all, these foods are an important part of our diet. Fruits and vegetables are one of the five major food groups. Every day, you should eat 3 to 5 servings of fruits and 3 to 5 servings of vegetables.

I also like helping my customers find what they need. People often ask me questions about how to cook fruits and vegetables. Some of their questions are hard. For example, do you know how to get the most vitamins out of a carrot? Wash it carefully. Then, eat the carrot raw—cooking takes some vitamins out.

Sometimes people want to know how to cook a vegetable without losing so many vitamins. For most vegetables, I suggest steam cooking. My favorite questions are from kids who want to know what to pack in their lunches. Which fruit do you think travels best in a lunch bag—an apple or a banana? I suggest the apple. It's less likely to get bruised or squashed.

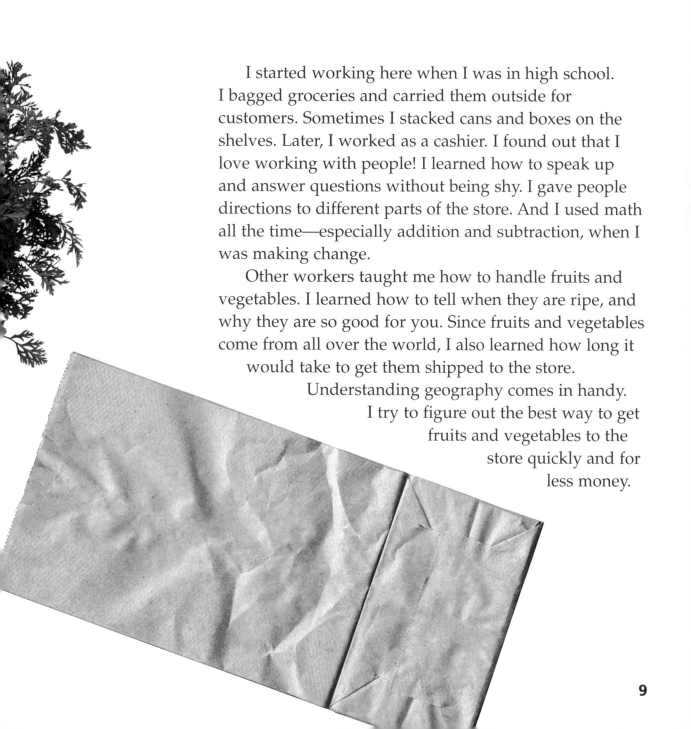

I started working here when I was in high school. I bagged groceries and carried them outside for customers. Sometimes I stacked cans and boxes on the shelves. Later, I worked as a cashier. I found out that I love working with people! I learned how to speak up and answer questions without being shy. I gave people directions to different parts of the store. And I used math all the time—especially addition and subtraction, when I was making change.

Other workers taught me how to handle fruits and vegetables. I learned how to tell when they are ripe, and why they are so good for you. Since fruits and vegetables come from all over the world, I also learned how long it would take to get them shipped to the store.

Understanding geography comes in handy. I try to figure out the best way to get fruits and vegetables to the store quickly and for less money.

9

It's my job to tell customers what I've learned about fruits and vegetables. I can explain how to cut up a pineapple, how long to cook broccoli, and how to eat an artichoke. If customers want to know what kind of apples would taste good in a salad, I'll give them some samples. Then, they can pick the kind of apples they like best. Sometimes, I let kids taste different fruits, so they can choose what to take in their lunch boxes.

I saw you point to the sign over the turnips. Then you said, "Yuck." Parsnips and turnips are less popular vegetables, but they are often used in delicious soups. Before the invention of refrigerators, people in cold climates often got through the winter months by eating root vegetables, which can stay fresh for a long time in a cold cellar. Lettuce and tomatoes were not part of their winter diet, because they could not stay fresh during a long trip from warmer regions.

Have you ever tasted jicama (**hee**-cah-mah)? or xigua (**she**-gwah)? or star fruit? I hadn't even heard of them before I started working here.

But my customers often ask me questions about these unusual kinds of produce. So I make sure to have answers for them. Jicama is a root, like a turnip. It grows in Mexico, Central America, and South America, and it tastes sweet and crunchy. Xigua is a Chinese watermelon. Star fruit is from Portugal, but it also grows in Asia and the Americas. Slices of star fruit look like stars, and they can taste sweet or sour.

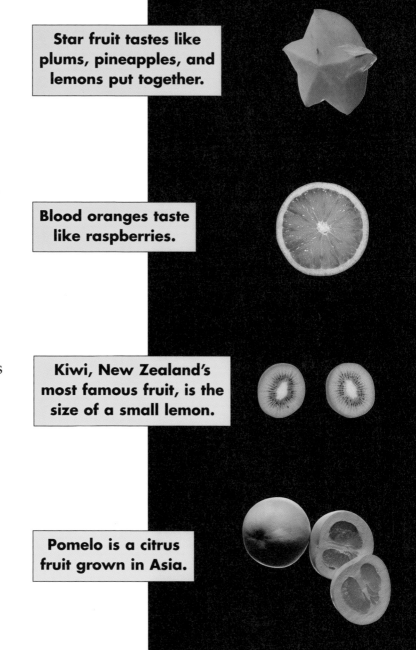

Star fruit tastes like plums, pineapples, and lemons put together.

Blood oranges taste like raspberries.

Kiwi, New Zealand's most famous fruit, is the size of a small lemon.

Pomelo is a citrus fruit grown in Asia.

Our store sells many different kinds of fruit and vegetables, but we don't have everything. Yesterday, a customer from China wanted to know if I could get her some kumquats (**come**-kwahts)—a tart fruit that looks like little oranges. I wrote "kumquats" in my notebook, along with her name and phone number. I looked up China in my atlas to see where it was. But then I discovered that kumquats are also grown in Florida and California in the United States. I ordered the kumquats from a distributor—a business that sells produce to stores like this one.

California

China

Florida

When you don't see me helping customers, I'm probably in the back of the store ordering things. Come on a little tour with me. I'll show you what goes on behind the scenes.

EMPLOYEES ONLY

Produce Manager

Here's my desk and computer. I use the computer to order fresh fruits and vegetables. I have to figure out how much produce I think customers will buy.

The owner of the store tells me how much money I can spend. I have to make a budget and spend the money wisely. I keep track of how much produce we usually sell each day, and I order extra things for holidays, like pumpkins at Thanksgiving.

I plan carefully, because I can't send the produce back if it doesn't get sold—I have to throw it away.

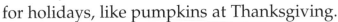

Later, I have to tell the owner how much we spent on produce and how much money we made selling it.

I use a computer to figure it all out. The computer helps me put information in columns and rows. This way I can add things up and get totals.

We also keep the produce back here before it goes out front. When the cartons of fruits and vegetables come in, we check them. I want to make sure I got what I ordered. I open the boxes and look at the fruits and vegetables to make sure they aren't damaged. I get plenty of exercise walking, standing, and bending. We use a special kind of cart to move the boxes. Some of them weigh more than 50 pounds!

Look at these boxes of bananas. You can see on the label that they came all the way from Mexico. Many fruits and vegetables come from the United States. Others travel from countries on the other side of the world.

PRODUCT OF MEXICO

No matter where the fruits and vegetables come from, they are all alike in one way. They are all parts of plants—leaves, stems, roots, seeds, fruits, or flowers. Sometimes the part of the plant that we cook and eat is the root, sometimes the seeds, and sometimes the fleshy part holding the seeds. For example, tomatoes and peaches, like many fruits, are the part of the plant that holds the seeds. Yes, tomatoes are considered fruit. Are you surprised?

There is a lot of science to be learned about the growing of produce. Most fruits grow on trees, bushes, and vines. They do not grow from seeds. Vegetables, however, do grow from seeds.

When the fruits and vegetables have grown enough, they can be harvested. Most fruits are picked by hand, but vegetables are usually harvested by machines. Some fruits, like bananas and tomatoes, are picked before they're ripe enough to eat. They ripen on their way to the store.

Workers wash the fruits and vegetables and pack them in boxes for the trip to the market. Some produce can be washed and packed by machines, but other produce must be packed by hand.

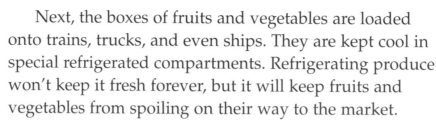

Next, the boxes of fruits and vegetables are loaded onto trains, trucks, and even ships. They are kept cool in special refrigerated compartments. Refrigerating produce won't keep it fresh forever, but it will keep fruits and vegetables from spoiling on their way to the market.

Sometimes, spiders and insects are accidentally packed up and carried with the produce. We watch out for spiders and insects when we unpack the produce.

At the end of their trip, the fruits and vegetables are unloaded into big buildings called warehouses. From there, other trucks take them to the stores that order them, like the one where I work.

As you can see, I wouldn't be able to stock the bins in our department with so many different fruits and vegetables without the help of the workers who drive trucks and run trains across the country. Because transportation in the United States is so fast and dependable, I can stock potatoes from Idaho, corn from Wisconsin, apples from Washington, and even pineapples from Hawaii, right here in this store.

Produce Manager

Every day, after the trucks deliver the produce, the other workers and I unpack it. Remember the customer who ordered the kumquats? I'll call her to tell her that her special fruit is here. Then, I'll help the workers stack the fruits and vegetables in baskets and on tables and counters. These stacks are called displays. I think they look beautiful!

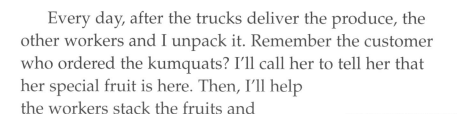

Fruits and vegetables should look mouth-watering so customers will buy them.

To make the displays look nice, we wash the produce before putting it out. That makes the colors look especially bright. We try to put contrasting colors next to each other. For example, I always put a bin of red apples between two bins of green ones. To make the displays look fuller, I sometimes put a small box in the bin and then stack the produce on top of it. That's better than stacking too much produce in one place, because the produce on the bottom of the stack could get squashed or bruised.

Produce Manager

The displays also make it easy for people to pick out the carrots, oranges, or peppers that they want. We have to be very careful with some kinds of produce, for example, tomatoes with stems. If we don't stack them just right, the hard stems can punch holes in the tomatoes.

We also have to be careful not to put potatoes under fluorescent lights. Those lights can make them turn green, which doesn't look very appealing. In the winter, we have to keep green bananas away from the door, because cold winds can turn them gray.

Keeping fruits and vegetables fresh is very important in my job. Nobody wants to buy limp lettuce or mushy bananas! My staff and I spend a lot of time checking the displays. For example, we check the ends of each head of lettuce for rusty stains. Only lettuce that is two or three days old would get those rusty stains. We also remove moldy fruit right away. Mold spreads fast, so all it takes is one moldy apple to ruin the whole display.

After we take away the old produce, we add new pieces of fruit and vegetables to keep the displays looking fresh. We are always careful to put the newest produce at the bottom of the display and the oldest on top. That's because the newer produce will stay fresh longer.

Throughout the day, the leafy produce, like lettuce and spinach, gets a shower! Special machines spray water on them to keep them fresh. Not all green vegetables are misted—I store the green beans far away from the sprayers because wet green beans tend to get brown spots. Sometimes, if I'm not too busy, I show kids how the sprayers work.

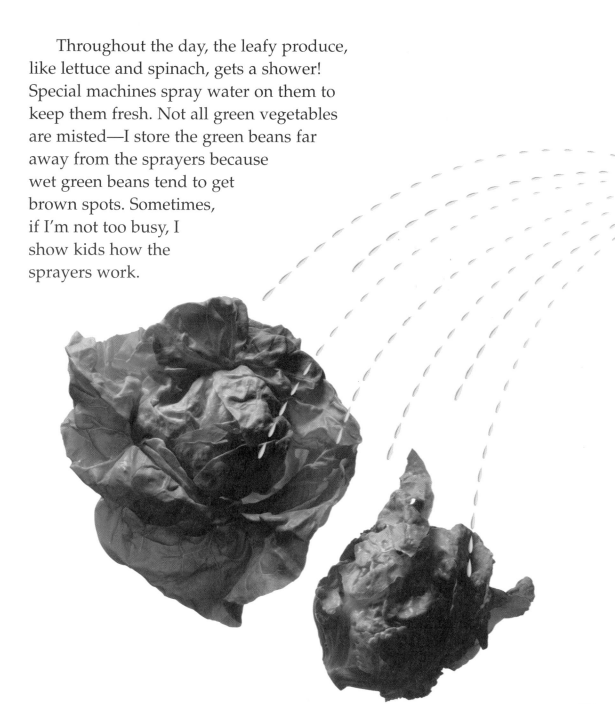

Produce Manager

When you visit the grocery store, you see signs everywhere. In the produce department, the signs tell how much the fruits and vegetables cost. I have to check the signs every day.

Sometimes I have to change the prices. If a big storm in California damages the lettuce crop, the farmers have less lettuce to sell. So the lettuce costs more money. In Michigan, the right amount of rain and warm weather may mean a big corn crop. Then, the corn will cost less money.

If prices go down far enough, we have a special sale to encourage our customers to buy the extra produce. You can buy a lot of food for not much money if you watch for signs like these: Three cucumbers for a dollar! Broccoli—89 cents a pound!

We sometimes make up packages of fruit and vegetables. Ann, one of my assistants, is doing this in the back of the store. She picks four ripe, undamaged peaches for each package. Then she puts them in a tray and wraps everything in clear plastic. To weigh the packages, Ann uses a special scale. It prints a label for each package that tells the name of the fruit, its weight, and its price.

The label also has a bar code on it that looks like zebra stripes. The stripes are arranged in a certain way to identify and track information. A machine at the checkout counter "reads" the bar codes and records the price of the package.

Ann

The salad bar is part of the produce department, too. We cut up the fruits and vegetables and get them ready to eat. Customers can use them to make salads to take home. We also make some mixed salads, like the carrot raisin salad. Although the rest of the store fills up in late afternoon, rush hour for the salad bar is lunch time! People who work at the businesses nearby come and get their lunches here.

I used to work in the salad bar. Now my friend Larry is in charge of it. He cuts up the fruits and vegetables. He makes the mixed salads, too.

Larry

Produce Manager

Larry washes his hands and puts on plastic gloves before he starts his work. He wipes the salad bar to keep it clean. Larry does these things to keep germs away from the food in the salad bar. We have a clear plastic shield over the top of the salad bar. It also helps to keep germs away from the food.

Everyone in the produce department is very careful not to spread germs. Before I became produce manager, I had to get a special letter from the state. It was like a health statement. It said that I learned the best ways to keep food preparation areas clean. I always tell my staff how important it is to wash their hands regularly and disinfect, or carefully clean, counters and food bins.

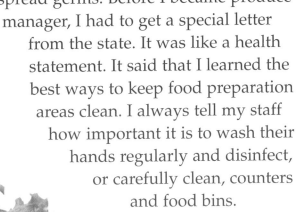

I taught Larry everything I know about the salad bar. Teaching is part of my job, too. When new workers start, I explain their jobs to them. I always show them what I want them to do, instead of just telling them. I teach them how to handle different kinds of fruits and vegetables. I remind them to handle tomatoes carefully so they don't bruise, for example.

Since I'm in charge of managing the produce department workers, I also have to plan their schedules. I figure out how many people need to work at each shift. When new jobs open up, I interview people and decide who is best for the job. I try to choose a person who is careful, dependable, and wants to learn new things.

I give directions to the workers in the produce department and make sure they do everything that needs to be done. That makes the produce department run smoothly, most of the time. Sometimes, problems come up, and I'm the person who has to solve them. For instance, it's my job to notice when aisles get blocked with boxes of fruits and vegetables and when something gets spilled where people could slip on it.

Spills and blocked aisles are safety problems, so
I make sure they get cleaned up right away. If
there is a long line at the checkout counter, I
go over there and help. I still have to answer
questions and help customers when I'm
checking shoppers out at the cash register.
Sometimes I look back at the end of the day
and can't even remember all the things I did!

It's hard work, but the other workers and I enjoy bringing the best fruits and vegetables to you and your family.

Next time you go to the supermarket, say "hi" to the produce workers. Ask some questions, if you want to.

And, when you take a bite of that sweet, juicy pear or apple you picked out, remember where it came from.

Think about all
the workers who
helped bring it
from the orchard
to your lunch box.

For More Information About Becoming a Produce Manager, Contact:
> Food Marketing Institute
> Publication and Video Sales Department
> 800 Connecticut Avenue, NW
> Washington, D.C. 20006

Produce Manager Education, Training, and Requirements:

Produce managers must have a high school diploma, and have experience working as a produce clerk or assistant manager. Some supermarkets require produce managers to have their county or state sanitary certificate. They must also understand produce ordering, inventory, pricing, and merchandising. Produce managers must be able to lift up to 50 pounds; unload trucks; and tolerate frequent walking, standing, bending, and reaching.

Related Careers:
> Grocery Store Manager
> Food Service Industry Worker
> Chef
> Waiter/Waitress
> Dietitian
> Nutrition Specialist in Hospital
> School Cafeteria Worker
> Day-care Program Food Preparer